Talking about

Our Environment

Malcolm Penny

RSVP
RAINTREE
STECK-VAUGHN
PUBLISHERS
A Steck-Vaughn Company

Austin, Texas

Titles in the series

Talking about

**Adoption • Alcohol • Bullying
Death • Disability • Drugs
Family Breakup • Our Environment**

Published by Raintree Steck-Vaughn Publishers,
an imprint of Steck-Vaughn Company

Library of Congress Cataloging-in-Publication Data
Powell, Jillian.
Environment / Jillian Powell.
      p.   cm.—(Talking about)
Includes bibliographical references and index.
Summary: Discusses the environment, what damage
has been done to it, and the things kids can do to help save it.
ISBN 0-8172-5889-2
1. Environment—Juvenile literature.
[1. Environment.]
I. Title. II. Series.

Printed in Italy. Bound in the United States.
1 2 3 4 5 6 7 8 9 0 03 02 01 00 99

Picture acknowledgments
Martyn F. Chillmaid cover (*main*), 4, 21, 26; Dennis Day cover (*background*); Ecoscene/ Ian Beames 6, /Frank Blackburn 17; ESA/PLI/Science Library 27; Eye Ubiquitous/ Roger Chester 19; Sally and Richard Greenhill 20, 25; Angela Hampton 7, 9, 10 (*top, bottom*), 11 (*top, bottom*), 12, 13, 14, 15, 16, 22, 23, 24; Tony Stone 8, 14, 18; Topham 5.

Contents

What is the environment?

The environment is all of the world we live in. It includes the air we breathe, the water we drink or swim in, the countryside around us, and the towns and cities where we live.

Today, the environment has some big problems. In some big cities the air is so dirty that people wear special masks.

What are the problems?

The whole world is getting warmer. This is called global warming. Air has also become polluted with chemicals.

Our factories and cars and some of the everyday things that we do, have all helped make these changes to the air we breathe.

These changes have caused other problems. The harmful rays of the sun can now reach us through the air.

You can use sun block or wear clothes to protect yourself from the sun.

What else damages our environment?

Even small actions can harm our environment. Dropping litter, painting graffiti on walls, or making loud noises all make life unpleasant for other people.

Little things, such as leaving the TV on at night or leaving a light on that you don't need, waste electricity, too.

If everyone thought about these things, life could be better for us all.

Samantha always keeps her candy wrappers in her pocket until she finds a place to put them.

9

How can we start to help?

Changes in the atmosphere are caused by industry and burning fuel. We buy the things industry makes and burn fuel to travel in our cars and to heat our homes.

Samantha and her friends decided to put their sweaters on rather than leave the heater on.

Vanessa and her parents walk with their shopping rather than using the car.

We cannot change everything we buy or stop using fuel, but we can think about the choices we make and their effect on the environment.

What can we do with garbage?

A lot of things are thrown away while they are still useful. Machines can sometimes be repaired instead of being replaced. Glass, plastic, tin, and paper can all be recycled.

Jim and Oliver collect bottles and jars and take them to be recycled.

Jim and Oliver also collect newspapers
and magazines at school.

How can we encourage recycling?

Paper towels, writing paper, envelopes, paper cups, and many other things are marked with a sign showing that they have been made from paper that has been recycled.

When we go shopping, we can look for this symbol and choose to buy recycled products.

Jim and Oliver hunt along the shelves
until they find recycled paper towels.

They tell their dad that it is ecofriendly
to buy these paper towels.

What else can we do when we go shopping?

Using our own bags or baskets instead of supermarket bags saves plastic. Reusing detergent containers and shampoo bottles also saves plastic.

Sally and Damon use their own shopping bags when they go shopping with their mother.

Labels tell us if the contents are ecofriendly. If we buy things made of wood, we can make sure they are from trees that will be replanted.

How can we save water?

The underground water supply is running out. Rain does not refill it properly, because too much runs off from roads and parking lots instead of soaking into the ground.

We can save water in many ways, such as by taking a shower instead of a bath or by turning off water while brushing our teeth.

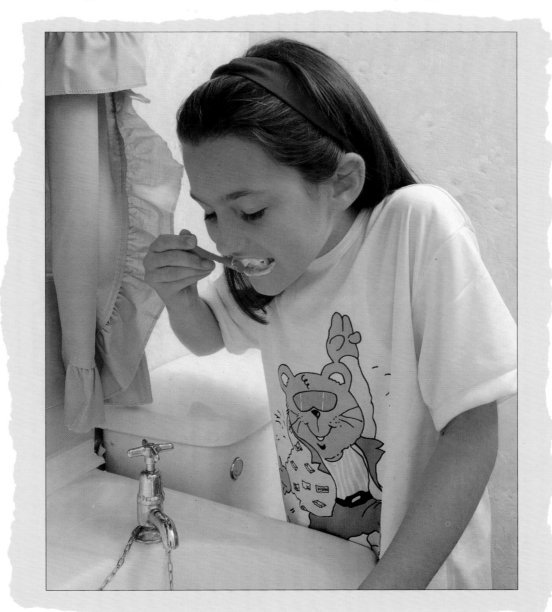

How can we save fuel?

We can save fuel by using public
transportation. One train or bus moves
more people than lots of cars. We can also
carpool with people we know.

If we want to make a short trip, to school or to stores, we could walk or ride a bike. Sean and Natalie's mother always rides her bike with them to school.

Can we stop pollution?

Gases from aerosols and old refrigerators can also pollute the atmosphere. Old refrigerators can be sent away to be safely emptied. New refrigerators use safer gases.

We can also use pump-action sprays instead of aerosols. John's dad used aerosol polish, but John told him it wasn't ecofriendly.

Now John's dad always uses pump-action sprays to polish or clean the house. His mother uses pump-action hair spray, too.

Can we help trees, plants and animals?

It is better to dig up weeds, because chemical weed-killers can harm wildlife. Planting a tree at school will provide a home for birds and insects.

Anna and her mother made a bird feeder at home. The birds like to eat scraps.

Daniel's class helped clean out a pond. Instead of garbage, they can now see fish and dragonflies.

Our wonderful world

A clean environment is good for everyone. Towns, cities, and the countryside can all be beautiful if we take care of them.

Small city parks and big national parks make life better for everybody and for plants and animals, too.

If everyone helps in a small way, we can solve the problems that threaten our environment and the world.

Notes for parents and teachers

Read this book with children one-on-one or in groups. Ask them what they like best about their immediate environment and what they think could be improved.

Discuss with them how many different kinds of environment there are, from large to small. Newspapers often write about the earth as a planet: this can be confusing to young people. Try starting on a much smaller scale, inside the home or, if possible, the backyard.

Even in large cities, parks and public spaces provide examples of shared environments. Visit these places together and try discussing what individuals can do to make life more pleasant for others. A railroad station or a bus station offers the chance to watch how people behave—as well as giving a demonstration of air pollution by fumes and smoke from gasoline.

Talk about choices in stores and supermarkets. Compare tissues or stationery made from recycled paper, for example, with those made from new materials. If the latter are found to be better, is the small loss of quality a price worth paying to protect the environment?

Environmental groups will be happy to supply information about their activities. Discuss with the children what each group does and whether it would be worth joining. Many of these organizations work at a local level, giving the chance to go along to watch what they do.

Encourage children to take an interest in the variety of living things that share our world. How many kinds of grass or beetles or wildflowers can we find in a garden or a park? It is not important at this stage to know the names of all the different kinds, but to observe that they are different.

Schools can encourage an understanding of simple ecology by setting up a flower garden or by growing a few vegetables such as beans or radishes. Let the children discover what these plants need to grow and extend the discussion to the wider world. This will also open up questions of organic farming as against the use of chemical weed-killers and pesticides.

Use stories in the press or on television to start discussions about the place of wildlife in the human world. The proposed introduction of wolves into certain areas in the United States or the release of mink from fur farms in the UK are good recent examples. TV wildlife documentaries also offer a good starting point for these discussions, for example, on the role of predators or the effects of fencing agricultural land.

The principal aim of this book is to show that small actions by individuals are as effective as major international agreements in helping to protect our environment.

Glossary

atmosphere The layer of air that covers the earth.

ecofriendly Something that does not harm the environment.

fuel Gasoline, diesel, coal, and natural gas are all fuels.

graffiti Things like people's names or rude words written or painted on walls.

industry All the companies that make things in factories.

polluted Made dirty.

public transportation Trains and buses, which can be used by everybody.

recycled Used again or made into something new instead of being thrown away.

Further information

Hall, Geoffrey. *Find Out About the Environment*. Jersey City, NJ: Parkwest Books, 1998.

Litvinoff, Miles. *The Young Gaia Atlas of Earthcare: An Illustrated Reference Guide to Looking After Our Planet*. New York: Facts on File, 1996.

Morichon, David. *Pollution? No Problem!* Ridgefield, CT: Millbrook Press, 1998.

Royston, Angela. *Recycling* (Environment Starts Here). Austin, TX: Raintree Steck-Vaughn, 1998.

Simon, Seymour. *Earth Words: A Dictionary of the Environment*. New York: HarperCollins, 1995.

Williams, Brenda. *Your Environment* (Geography Starts Here). Austin, TX: Raintree Steck-Vaughn, 1999.

Index